W9-BBC-376

DATE DUE

After Suicide

Living With the Questions

by Eileen Kuehn

Consultant:
Roderick W. Franks, MA, LSW
Licensed Psychologist
Hennepin County Family Court Services
Minneapolis, Minnesota

Grief and Loss

LifeMatters
an imprint of Capstone Press
Mankato, Minnesota

c 1   2003   15.95

LifeMatters Books are published by Capstone Press
PO Box 669 • 151 Good Counsel Drive • Mankato, Minnesota 56002
http://www.capstone-press.com

Printed in the United States of America

Library of Congress Cataloging-in-Publication Data
Kuehn, Eileen.
      After suicide: living with the questions / by Eileen Kuehn.
           p.   cm. — (Grief and loss)
      Includes bibliographical references and index.
      ISBN 0-7368-0748-9
      1. Grief in adolescence—Juvenile literature. 2. Bereavement in adolescence—Juvenile literature. 3. Loss (Psychology) in adolescence—Juvenile literature. 4. Teenagers and death—Juvenile literature. [1. Suicide.] I. Title. II. Series.
      BF724.3.G73 K82 2001
      362.28´3—dc21   00-010629
                                                            CIP

      Summary: Defines suicide and its effects on teen survivors of someone who dies by suicide. Describes who dies by suicide and why, as well as the stages of grieving a loss through suicide. Provides ways teens can cope and heal and ways to help someone else who experiences another person's suicide.

Staff Credits
Charles Pederson, editor; Adam Lazar, designer; Kim Danger, photo researcher

Photo Credits
Cover: UPmagazine/©Tim Yoon
©Artville/Clair Alaska, 17, 33, 37, 39; Don Carstens, 7, 49
International Stock/©Roger Markham Smith, 22; ©Michael Ventura, 29; ©Patrick Ramsey, 45, 51;
©Bill Stanton, 47
©PhotoDisc, 13
Photri, Inc./©Skjold 9, 55
Unicorn Stock Photos/©Robert W. Ginn, 19
Uniphoto Picture Agency, 40
UPmagazine/©Tim Yoon, 59
Visuals Unlimited/©Mark S. Skalny, 57

A 0 9 8 7 6 5 4 3 2 1

Table of Contents

- Survivors of someone who dies by suicide often wonder why the suicide happened.

- People of all ages, races, and cultures die by suicide. It's the third leading cause of death in the United States for young people between ages 15 and 24.

- The most common ways to die by suicide are using guns, hanging, jumping from high places, and taking poison. Drowning or inhaling motor vehicle exhaust are other common methods.

- Many different reasons can lead someone to die by suicide. Usually suicide occurs for a combination of reasons. There are signs you can watch for if someone is considering suicide.

- Depression is the main cause of suicide.

Chapter 1

The Haunting Question: "Why?"

Suicide occurs when people intentionally kill themselves. Sometimes, people try to kill themselves but don't succeed. This is called attempted suicide. Suicide is terrible for people who knew the person who has died. In this book, the people who are left behind after someone dies by suicide are called survivors. For these suicide survivors, the first question is usually, "Why did she or he do it?"

Even if it's someone you knew only slightly, you might wonder why. It's normal after a suicide to examine possible reasons for it. But no matter how much we learn, the question of why can never totally be answered. We can never know exactly what was in the mind of the person who died by suicide. Even the few people who leave notes may not give true reasons for their suicide. Suicide survivors are left to ask their own questions. Why did she do it? How will I live without him? Was she depressed? Why didn't he ask for help?

Did You Know?

At least 4.4 million people in the United States are suicide survivors.

Sean, Age 16

After Sean's parents divorced when he was 8, Sean's mother got a job as a nurse. Sean helped around the house. They cleaned and did a lot of other things together. In high school, Sean made the football team. He had a lot of friends. He studied hard to get good grades. His mother had encouraged him and told him how proud of him she was. Then she used drugs to kill herself. She must have gotten them from the hospital where she worked, Sean thought. He supposed he'd never know why she killed herself. "Didn't she care about me? She said she did, but maybe she lied."

Who Dies by Suicide?

Sean's mother didn't seem like someone who would kill herself. It's not always easy to say who will die by suicide. Every year, more than 30,000 Americans of all cultures, races, and ages take their own life. Suicide is the third leading cause of death in the United States for young people between the ages of 15 and 24. Every year, more than 5,000 young people kill themselves.

Up to four times more girls than boys attempt suicide. However, four times more boys than girls actually succeed. Boys are more likely to kill themselves quickly by crashing their car or shooting or hanging themselves. Until recently, girls were more likely to use slower methods such as taking pills or slashing their wrists. They were likely to be discovered and saved from death and so not complete the suicide. However, recently, girls have been using guns in equal numbers to boys.

American Indians in the United States have the highest rate of suicide. American Indian teens often experience cultural confusion. This means that they feel they don't fit in anywhere. This may be because the U.S. culture expects American Indian teens to live like white Americans. Yet their American Indian heritage calls strongly to them.

Almost one-third of all teen suicides are by gay and lesbian teens. They often face the continuous stress of keeping their identity secret. Frequently, they receive little support from family or friends when they come out. They may also be called names or be beaten or harrassed. Ongoing stresses like these may lead to depression and finally to suicide.

It's estimated that 30 to 50 percent of teens use alcohol or other drugs before killing themselves. These substances confuse judgment and reinforce negative thinking and anger.

Did You Know?

Reported suicides may be only one-fourth the number of actual suicides. Some deaths reported as car accidents, heart attacks, and accidental alcohol or other drug overdoses may really be suicides. There may be many reasons for this. For example, only about 20 to 30 percent of those who kill themselves leave a note. And in some states, a sudden death isn't considered suicide unless the person leaves a note. Sometimes investigators don't find a suicide note because a friend or relative may have destroyed it. This may occur because some people believe insurance companies won't pay life insurance policies if someone dies by suicide.

Methods of Suicide

People kill themselves in many ways, but several methods are most common. Guns account for more than half of all suicides. People also may complete suicide by jumping from high places or taking poison. Hanging, drowning, or breathing motor vehicle exhaust are other methods.

What Triggers Suicide?

Some people would prefer to be able to point at a single reason for all suicides. However, no one reason can explain every suicide. Usually a person chooses suicide because risk factors or challenges pile up. It's common to find several risk factors when someone dies by suicide, such as those listed on the next page.

- Depression

- Grief at someone's death

- Failure to achieve an important goal

- Trouble with the law

- An unplanned pregnancy

- Breakup of a romantic relationship

- Divorce

- Isolation from others, or feeling alone

- Conflicts with family members

- Criticism from friends or family

- History of suicide in the family

- Influence from reports of other suicides

One of these reasons may have triggered suicide for some people.
But suicide usually occurs because several factors combine to
pressure a person to take his or her own life.

Teen Talk

"I can't think. I want to sink into sleep, to escape. I'm so tired. To care about anything takes such a tremendous effort. Everything's mixed up. The fog keeps rolling in. I want the world to leave me alone, but it slips in through the cracks . . . I can't handle it much longer . . ."—LaVon, age 17, in a diary entry made shortly before she killed herself

Suicidal Signs

The following are indicators that a person may be considering suicide. As with the suicide triggers, only one or two signs doesn't mean someone definitely is considering suicide. It does mean that you should watch for other signs.

- Throwing or giving away favorite possessions

- Putting personal affairs in order

- Talking about suicide or dying; for example, "I won't be a problem to you much longer." "Nothing matters." "It's no use." "I won't see you again." "I want to kill myself."

- Becoming suddenly cheerful after a period of being sad or withdrawn

- Being interested in death, reading or asking questions about it

- Taking needless risks such as driving recklessly or using alcohol or other drugs

- Showing any signs of depression

Depression

The main cause of suicide is depression. It can be a long-lasting mental illness in which a person feels extremely sad, empty, hopeless, or alone. It's a medical illness like cancer or heart disease. However, instead of affecting the heart or lungs, it affects the brain and nervous system.

Depression is one of the most common mental health problems facing North Americans today. More than one in five U.S. citizens experiences it during their life. Every year, 17 million people are diagnosed with depression. About 12 percent of U.S. teens have it.

In the United States, 15 percent of people with depression complete the act of suicide. An even higher percentage attempts suicide. Suicide often occurs when sadness and unclear thinking are part of depression. Depression almost always can be treated successfully.

Causes of Depression

It's hard to pinpoint a single cause for depression. In some people, one or several factors can contribute to it. In other people, depression develops for no apparent reason.

An imbalance of chemicals in the brain may cause depression. Factors leading to depression may be stress, substance use, inherited tendencies, emotional shock, or grief. Illnesses such as cancer, heart disease, or Parkinson's disease can trigger a clinical depression.

Fast Fact

Most people who die by suicide tell someone beforehand.

Signs of Depression

Signs of depression may include any of the following:

- Excessive crying or a feeling of emptiness

- Feelings of hopelessness or guilt

- Changes in eating and sleeping habits

- Withdrawal from friends and family

- Lack of interest in activities that previously were enjoyed

- Violent actions, rebellious behavior, or running away

- Neglect of personal appearance

- Major change in personality

- Boredom or lack of concentration

- Stomachaches, headaches

- Chronic, or long-lasting, fatigue

- Abuse of alcohol or other drugs

- Thoughts about death or suicide, or attempting suicide

People may be able to live with depression if they feel hopeful
that things will get better. But when there is no hope, suicide may
seem like the only way out. You may know someone with these
pressures or signs of depression or suicidal behavior. If so, tell a
trusted adult right away.

Points to Consider

- Why do you think someone might commit suicide? Explain.

- What are some reasons why a person might think about killing
  himself or herself?

- If you thought someone you knew might try to kill himself or
  herself, whom could you tell? List these people.

○ Suicide survivors may develop depression, post-traumatic stress disorder, and even thoughts of suicide themselves.

○ Suicide is hard for survivors to handle. The pain they feel is like no other pain.

○ Survivors must deal with many intense feelings including shock, shame, denial, guilt, anger, and sadness.

○ Mourning is a state in which survivors try to accept a suicide.

○ Survivors may feel shame as they deal with a person's suicide. Shame comes from negative attitudes and superstitions about suicide. In past years, people who died by suicide were considered outcasts. Their families were punished for the suicide.

Suicide Survivors: The Ones Left to Cope

Effects of Suicide on a Survivor

The emotional pain after a suicide may cause survivors to feel severely depressed and hopeless. The suicide rate for survivors is eight times higher than the suicide rate for other people.

Suicide survivors often must deal with greater guilt, shame, and rejection than do survivors of other deaths. As a result, suicide survivors sometimes develop serious mental problems. These problems may include depression and post-traumatic stress disorder (PTSD). This includes feelings that may occur long after a person has been exposed to violence or severe stress.

Sometimes suicide survivors begin having problems with abuse of alcohol or other drugs. They may not be able to get along with their friends and family.

Physical symptoms such as headaches and stomachaches are common for suicide survivors. These people also may have trouble sleeping or eating or may live with constant anxiety.

Did You Know?

Dante Alighieri was an Italian poet who lived almost 700 years ago. He wrote a poem called "The Inferno." He pictured hell as having rings, with one of the most terrible rings for those who had died by suicide. They were sent to the seventh circle of hell and turned into bleeding trees. The souls of those who died by suicide then were eaten by harpies, who were birdlike monsters.

Mariel, Age 15

Mychal died in a car accident three weeks ago, just after Mariel broke up with him. She tried to be kind when she told him he'd changed and they couldn't be together anymore. He was always angry and unhappy. Nothing she did or said seemed to cheer him up. He stormed out after she broke up with him. "You're just like everyone!" he yelled at her. "No one cares!"

His death was a terrible shock. Mariel was still numb. "It's my fault he died," she thought. "If we hadn't broken up, Mychal would still be alive!"

Going On

The sting of death is "less sharp for the person who dies than it is for the bereaved [grieving] survivors," wrote a famous scholar, Arnold Toynbee. When a person dies by suicide, the survivors must pick up the pieces of life and go on. Survivors of suicide are left to deal with many painful feelings.

Bereavement

In bereavement, the survivor first experiences the shock and grief of the suicide. Bereavement involves a variety of emotions. Many of these same emotions may occur after an unsuccessful suicide attempt. A survivor can begin to grieve while bereaved. Grieving is the process of working through feelings of loss. Chapter 3 discusses the grieving process.

Shock

Shock is often the first feeling experienced during bereavement. During shock, your mind sometimes goes numb. It may seem to shut off for a while. Some things become hard to remember. It's common to experience flashbacks, or images of the person as he or she was before the suicide.

Shock actually may be positive. It's the mind's way of dulling the pain. While in shock, the mind lets only a small amount of reality filter in. This can help a person adjust slowly to the suicide.

Shame

The feeling of shame makes some people lie about the cause of death. Families sometimes build up an untrue story about the person who has died by suicide. After a while this story may seem to be true. However, covering up a suicide is less common now than it was years ago.

Denial

Denying that the suicide happened is another way people may cope while bereaved. Some people may insist that the suicide was an accident. For example, they may know the person died by firing a pistol into his or her mouth. But they can't accept that fact. Feelings of shame also may trigger denial. People may never know exactly what was in the mind of the person who died by suicide.

Guilt

Suicide survivors often have greater guilt than they would with other kinds of death. They may believe they should have seen the suicide coming. They may think they could have done something to prevent it.

Some suicide survivors feel guilty because they think they weren't good enough to the person. Some survivors may feel relief that the person no longer is in pain. Then they may feel even more guilty at their relief. Some people may blame suicide survivors for not having done more to prevent the suicide.

Remember Mariel? Guilt has overwhelmed her. She believes Mychal killed himself because she broke up with him. Mariel has a form of guilt that may harm her. People with such strong guilt may want to seek help from a doctor or counselor.

Anger

Suicide survivors often are angry. Survivors may feel angry at themselves for not stopping the suicide. They may want to blame something or someone else for not stopping it. Suicide survivors often become angry with the person who died.

Sadness

Suicide survivors often feel sadness as well as the other emotions discussed here. This sadness takes many forms. Some survivors show their sadness through sobbing or screaming. Others may show it by becoming silent and withdrawn. It's important for survivors to let this sadness out in helpful ways.

Mourning

After grief feelings pass, people usually move to the next state of being, called mourning. This is when survivors try to accept the suicide.

The process of mourning someone's suicide is likely to be more difficult than mourning a normal death. There's the added burden of trying to understand why the suicide occurred.

Teen Talk

"I'm so ashamed to tell people my mom killed herself. It's easier to say she had an accident. You don't have to get into that whole explanation."—Lin, age 14

"When my father killed himself, my family said it was a heart attack. The truth was that he went to a bar after work and got drunk. Then he drove out on a lonely country road and shot himself with his hunting rifle. I saw him putting it in the truck the day before he killed himself."—Rosita, age 13

The Stigma of Suicide

A suicide survivor may have extra problems because of the stigma of suicide. Stigma is shame and judgment. In this case, it's placed on those who die by suicide and sometimes on their family. For many years, if someone did die by suicide, their family was shamed and punished. The stigma of suicide has started to fade only in the last 10 to 20 years.

If someone attempted suicide as recently as the 1960s and 1970s, the family often hid it from others. A completed suicide often was covered up and called an accident. Sometimes people may have tried to hide a suicide by saying it was a disease. For example, instead of suicide, a family might have said the person died from heart disease.

After Suicide

Every 17 minutes in America, someone dies by suicide. Every day worldwide, more than 1,000 people die by suicide.

Suicide Superstitions

Much of the shame around suicide comes from superstitions. In the past, many people believed that evil spirits lived in the body of a person who had died by suicide. In some places, the body of those who killed themselves was buried at night or at a crossroads. The traffic over the crossroads was supposed to keep the body down. In Massachusetts hundreds of years ago, cartloads of stones were piled on the grave of people who killed themselves.

In the 1300s in Europe, a stake often was driven through the heart of people who killed themselves. People from Finland never touched the corpse of a person who died by suicide. The corpse was lifted into a coffin with fire pokers. People feared that disease or the "curse of suicide" would take over the family.

Until the 1900s, many groups usually had no funeral for a person who died by suicide. The grave was often outside a regular cemetery. In France in the late 1600s, the body often was dragged through the streets and then hanged. French law said the body had to be thrown in a sewer or the city dump.

A Final Good-Bye

Today, people look for answers about how to go on without the person who has killed himself or herself. One way to resolve some of their feelings is with a funeral. This is a special ceremony that allows family and friends to say good-bye to the dead. The funeral often helps to make the death a reality to survivors. It likely will be sad, but it's the time when healing can begin.

A funeral provides an opportunity for mourners to accept someone's death. This is one of the first steps in the grieving process.

Did You Know?

The danger of suicide is not over when a troubled person starts to look or feel better. Most suicides happen within three months after the person starts to feel better.

Points to Consider

- Do you know anyone who is a suicide survivor? What kinds of feelings did they go through? Did they experience depression or post-traumatic stress disorder, or have thoughts of suicide themselves?

- How do you think suicide is like or unlike other kinds of death?

- What do you think are some of the feelings a survivor might experience after a suicide?

- Do you think suicide has a stigma attached to it? Why or why not?

- A death from suicide can make the grieving process more difficult than for other kinds of death. People may be shocked or stunned. They have many questions about why the suicide happened.

- Grieving is necessary. It must be handled by working through painful thoughts and feelings as they come up.

- The grieving process is different for every person. Dealing with grief can take years. Dealing with suicide is different from working through other forms of grief.

- The grieving process usually consists of three major phases: avoidance, confrontation, and accommodation. Each phase has its own set of feelings or emotions.

- Working through the grieving process can help you grow as a person.

Grieving: Dealing With the Pain and Loss

Charles, Age 15

Charles's 13-year-old brother, Mickey, killed himself with the gun kept in their father's desk drawer. Charles blames himself and his parents. "Why did Dad keep that gun loaded?" he says angrily.

Charles knew Mickey had become sad and hard to get along with in the past year. Charles tried to ignore Mickey as much as he could. "If only I'd spent more time with Mickey, he'd probably be here today," Charles says.

Charles tortures himself with dozens of things he thinks he should have done. Now it's too late. His brother is dead. "I wish I had that gun," he thinks to himself. "I feel like killing myself."

Some people find it helps to talk with others about the person who has died. Sharing the pain of death can help the healing to begin. Others prefer not to talk about the suicide. They find it easier to talk about ordinary things in life. In either case—talking or not talking about the suicide—friends and family need to respect each person's choice.

Suicide Survivor Grief

Dealing with suicide grief is different from other forms of grieving. A suicide survivor may feel responsible for somehow failing the person who has died. Sometimes a death by suicide sets off agonizing guilt, anger, and self-blame.

Death by suicide forces many people into second-guessing themselves. Second-guessing happens frequently for suicide survivors. A sure sign of second-guessing is that "if only" creeps into thoughts and conversation. "If only I'd talked to her more." Or as Charles says, "If only I'd spent more time with Mickey."

Suicide can raise unexpected emotions. It's common to feel rejected or abandoned by the person who has died. The feeling of abandonment may trigger intense anger. Sometimes it takes a long time for these feelings to fade.

Grieving Is Necessary

Grieving a death by suicide is a process that a survivor must go through. It's a time of learning to live without the person.

To grieve in a way that's helpful, you need to feel your pain and recognize your emotions. In this way, suicide survivors can begin to rebuild their life.

"It's weird, you know, to lose a friend because your father killed himself. After the funeral, my friend never called anymore. We just went our separate ways. I don't think he knew what to say to me. The whole thing just freaked him out."—Stevie, age 15

People often are impatient about grieving. They want it to be over right away. But there's no fast way to work through grieving. Trying to pretend the suicide never happened won't help you work through your grief faster. When painful thoughts and emotions come up, they must be dealt with. Grieving and its emotions can continue for years—sometimes throughout life.

Grieving varies from person to person, but it does have a general timetable. Usually, the first two months are the worst. Some people feel the pain right away. Other people may feel numb before they can feel the pain. At some point, the pain may feel like a dull ache that comes and goes. However, it may never completely go away. Part of helpful grieving is learning to live with that ache.

Grieving Phases

Some experts say the grieving process has several phases. Each phase involves a separate reaction to a suicide. The three phases are avoidance, confrontation, and accommodation.

Realize that a phase lasts until you've worked through it. A phase may take more time for some people than for others. This is especially true when people grieve a suicide.

Avoidance

Avoidance is the first phase of grieving. It's when a person tries to pretend the death didn't happen. During the avoidance phase, you may feel confused. You might not be able to understand what has happened or make sense of anything. Some things that go with this phase of grieving are:

o Shock

o Denial

o Emotional anesthesia, or inability to feel emotions

Shock, one form of avoidance, may cause your mind to feel numb. Denial is another form of avoidance. In some ways, denial is good. It's the body's way of helping to understand death a little at a time. A person may deny the emotions that come with someone's suicide but still be able to feel other emotions. Emotional anesthesia is slightly different from denial. It's a complete loss of the ability to feel any emotions.

Confrontation

The second phase of grieving is confrontation. This phase may happen at the funeral or at some other time. This is when you acknowledge that the person has died. But you might still want to reach out to him or her. You may remember good and bad times you spent with the person.

The suicide becomes real to the survivor in this phase. Sadness and the feeling of loss may be at their strongest. For example, you may feel as if you can't stop sobbing or control your anger. The strength of these feelings helps you confront the reality of death. It's painful, but each time this feeling occurs, you move forward in the grieving process.

During the confrontation phase, you may feel extremely angry or overwhelmingly sad. You might feel that the person has abandoned you. Many confusing reactions typically occur and may come at moments when you least expect them.

Delia, Age 16

Delia had been thinking about her best friend, Cary, a lot. Cary had been dead for eight months. She had smashed her car into a tree. Her death was ruled accidental, but Delia didn't believe it.

Now, a cloudy, gray feeling washed over Delia like a huge wave. It came, stayed awhile, then went away. But lately the feeling was coming more often and staying longer. It was like the feelings Cary told her about before she died.

Delia tried to tell her parents about her feelings, but they said, "It's just something teens go through. Think positive, and you'll feel better tomorrow."

"I can't stand it anymore," Delia said to herself. "Why am I even alive? My life is terrible." She wanted to be with Cary. "I'm going for a car ride," she told her mother. "Good-bye."

Delia is confronting her grief. She knows Cary is dead, but she can't get beyond that fact. Instead, Delia is thinking about killing herself. Thoughts of suicide sometimes happen to a survivor who is stuck in the grief.

If this happens, it's vitally important to seek help. If a parent doesn't see how deep the survivor's pain is, it may be necessary to ask a professional grief counselor for help. A grief counselor is trained to help a survivor learn to accept a suicide.

It's important to realize that grieving people can experience depression. Chapter 1 discussed some signals of depression. If you see those signals in yourself or other survivors, tell a trusted adult as soon as possible.

Accommodation

The third phase of grieving is accommodation. This is a gradual acceptance of the suicide. You learn to live without the person who died by suicide. You may notice fewer instances of the sharp, confrontational grief.

At this time, grieving can become less painful. Slowly, you might feel like getting on with your life. Life can't go back to the way it was before the suicide. However, you can learn to handle life as it is. The sadness and hurting slowly can fade as you relearn to live in a world that no longer includes the person.

Suicide survivors may continue to have feelings of guilt because they are still living. Survivors may feel bad about being alive while the other person is dead. Survivors may feel guilty when they have fun.

Accommodation is generally the longest phase of the grieving process. It can take years, depending on who is grieving. Death by suicide may increase the length of each phase of grieving.

It's also likely that as teens get older, they may understand the suicide differently. They might need to work through the phases again in a different way. Some of the negative feelings may stay with a survivor throughout life. That's okay. The goal isn't to get rid of the feelings but to be able to live with them in a healthy way.

Growing as a Person

Grieving can help you grow and mature as a person. Working through the grieving process can give you a better understanding of yourself. You may learn to make wiser choices. You may learn to value your own life more.

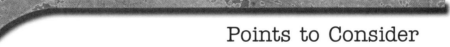

Points to Consider

- Why do you think survivors sometimes blame themselves for suicide?

- A leading expert in dealing with death says that as we understand more about death, we learn about life. What do you think this means?

- Why do you think suicide tears some families apart while other families grow closer?

- How might grieving help you grow and mature? Explain.

- Doing grief work is necessary to heal the sadness of the mind, body, and soul.

- Suicide survivors can begin to grieve helpfully through grief work activities.

- Support groups and counseling are two ways to get help with your pain.

Chapter 4

Healing Tools for Suicide Survivors

Lourdes, Age 16

Lourdes awoke early. Raoul had killed himself two months ago today. Raoul was Lourdes's best friend since childhood. Their life together came crashing down when Raoul killed himself. It was a total surprise to Lourdes. She hadn't thought Raoul's moodiness would lead to his dying.

For the first weeks after his death, Lourdes felt like a lump of stone, unable to feel anything. Then her mother insisted she see a grief counselor. The counselor suggested that Lourdes get up early every morning to do grief work. This would help her deal with her feelings and work through her grief. It was planned almost to be like homework.

Some of the work was hard. Some of it made her cry. But it seemed to help. "I don't think about Raoul every minute of every day. After I do my grief work, it's sort of like I've let go of some of the hurtful thoughts," she said.

Teen Talk

"Sometimes I get so angry that my cousin killed herself that I can hardly stand it. When I get that angry feeling, I have to find something to do. I start cleaning the house and don't quit until I can't work anymore."—Frank, age 14

"After my boyfriend left me, I slashed my wrists. I thought I wanted to die. But now I'm glad I didn't. I would have missed out on a lot of things."—Lee, age 15

Grief Work

When someone dies by suicide, it's necessary to deal with the sadness you feel. A way to do this is by doing grief work. This is working through your grief instead of just waiting for it to fade.

Lourdes has found productive ways to cope with her loss. She still needs to work on her grief for a while. But she has accepted Raoul's death and is on her way to rebuilding her life.

Suicide survivors are the only ones who can do their own grief work. No one else can feel the feelings necessary to recover from someone's suicide. However, it may help the process to do grief work with a friend or family member.

You can do many things while working on grief. First, set aside time each day in a separate place. That will give you privacy to think about the person being grieved. Plan to spend 15 to 30 minutes each day doing grief work.

One of Lourdes's first projects was to remember Raoul in a true way. The counselor explained that when a person misses a loved one, the person might remember only the good things. The grieving process is delayed when a person begins thinking of the person who died as perfect.

The counselor had Lourdes draw a line down the center of a piece of paper. She labeled the columns "Good" and "Not so good." Then in each column, she listed as many things as she could about Raoul. "This will help you understand your true relationship with Raoul," the counselor said.

Grief Work Activities

If you're not seeing a counselor, you might want to make a contract with yourself. You can agree to do grief work every day as long as it seems necessary. You may do this alone or with a friend or family member. Lourdes's first assignment was one example of grief work. There are many others such as those described here.

Mind-Mapping

You probably have done mind-mapping in school. In the middle of a piece of paper, write the name of the person who died by suicide. Draw a circle around the name. Then draw a line in any direction and another circle at the end. In the second circle, write the first word that comes to mind about the person. Keep adding circles with words. Repeat this process for 10 or 15 minutes. This can help you find your true feelings about the person.

Journal Writing

Many people keep a journal during the grieving process. A journal is simply a collection of pages that you can write in. It can be as simple or fancy as you like. Use a journal to write what you think and feel about the person who died. For example, you may wish to tell the person how you felt when he or she died. Or you might want to write your feelings in the form of a letter to the person.

Writing in a journal can help you sort out your feelings. You may feel relief by writing about the hurt, anger, and pain. Once you have written your thoughts, they often lose their intensity. They may lose their power to stay in your mind constantly.

Making Lists

Lourdes listed things about Raoul that she thought were good and not so good. You can make other kinds of lists. For example, divide a sheet of paper into columns. At the top of each, write emotions such as *sad, afraid,* or *angry.* Under each emotion, write whatever comes to mind. For example: "I'm afraid to think about your suicide." "I'm angry that you left me."

When you've finished, tear up your list and throw it away. Imagine that you're getting rid of your negative feelings with the scraps of paper.

Other Grief Work

Some other helpful ways of working through grief can include the following:

- Play or listen to music.

- Burn candles, incense, or herbs in your own grief ritual.

- Dance, paint, or sketch your feelings.

- Do kind things for other people.

- Exercise regularly. Take a long walk or run.

- Let out your feelings in safe ways and places. For example, pound or scream into a pillow. Sing, play sad songs, laugh, cry, or yell.

- Have fun. Go to parties or do a hobby you enjoy.

- Meditate.

- Read.

Ask for Help

While it's possible to help yourself, many people find that the best healing comes when they have help. Family and friends have been metioned as a source of support. There are other places you can find help as a survivor of suicide.

Support Groups

A support group consists of people who share a problem. Alcoholics Anonymous is a support group you may have heard of. People meet in support groups to share feelings or ideas. Often, a trained professional leads these groups. There are many benefits of support groups. You might be surprised to learn that others also feel guilt, anger, confusion, shame, fear, or depression.

There are a number of ways to find a support group for suicide survivors. One is to contact one of the organizations listed on pages 60 and 61 of this book. Ask for the name of a local suicide survivor's support group. You also might call a local crisis telephone line or suicide hot line. Or try your local community mental health center. Look for resources advertised in your school or community. This may include support groups and teen help lines.

Counseling

When you're in pain, you may need the help of a trained professional. Don't rule out the relief counseling can bring.

Your parents may have insurance that requires you to pick from certain counselors. If possible, get a recommendation about one of them. Do you know another teen who goes to one of them? Ask if that teen respects and likes the counselor. Or ask a parent, a favorite teacher, or a school counselor to recommend someone.

If you can, talk with the counselor first. It's a good way to tell if you like the person. Pay attention to your feelings when you talk with the counselor. Does the counselor accept you or seem to want to change you? Do you feel comfortable or anxious? If you feel anxious, pay attention to that feeling and decide if you want to find someone else.

Points to Consider

- Can you think of some helpful ways to express anger or sadness about the suicide of someone you knew? What are they?

- Do you think it helps to list the good and not-so-good qualities of someone who dies by suicide? Explain.

- What grief work examples might you try if a friend died by suicide?

- Is it a good idea to interview a counselor before you begin working with him or her? Why or why not?

○ Talking about a suicide with a professional counselor can help survivors sort out their feelings.

○ Professional grief programs called postvention programs often are set up in schools or the community after a student's suicide. They help suicide survivors work through grief in helpful ways.

○ Postvention programs help to discourage the idea of cluster suicides. These programs help students adjust to a suicide of a classmate.

○ Over time, unresolved grief can cause serious disease and depression.

○ When someone dies by suicide, the pattern of the survivors' life changes. Nothing works as it used to. Survivors must relearn life and do things in ways that don't include the person who died by suicide.

After Suicide

Getting Professional Help

Experts say that talking about suicide is one of the best things anyone can do. By talking about the feelings that a suicide brings, those feelings can be released.

Postvention Programs

If a student dies by suicide, many schools or communities immediately organize grief programs to help classmates survive the loss. Grief counselors are available to talk with individuals or groups of students. These are called postvention programs.

Suicide survivors can talk through their fears and feelings with counselors. They tell students it's okay to have anger, fear, shame, guilt, and other emotions. The counselors can help students work through those feelings and learn to live with them in a healthy way.

Jamie, Age 14

Jamie and her friends Chantell and Celine were out of their minds with grief. Robin, another friend, had killed herself two days ago. "We think we pushed her into it," Jamie told the grief counselor who came to their school. "We tried to get Robin to dump her boyfriend." The friends had told Robin that they saw him with another girl.

Jamie, Chantell, and Celine couldn't face anyone and even talked about killing themselves. "We're so ashamed that we were mean to Robin," Jamie told the counselor. "We just wanted Robin to get rid of that creep. He wasn't good for her."

The counselor explained that Jamie and her friends had no reason to feel guilty. "You didn't kill Robin. You were trying to help her. Be proud that you were good friends to her," the counselor said. He went on, "A person who kills himself or herself has disturbed feelings. There usually are many reasons for a suicide. Robin had other obstacles in her life besides her boyfriend."

The girls met several times with the counselor. "We felt better afterward," Jamie said later. "Everything was bottled up inside us and ready to explode. But after we started talking about it, we decided suicide wasn't for us. People who feel like taking their own life really need to talk with someone like our counselor first. Maybe then they'd change their mind about suicide."

After Suicide

Cluster Suicides

One main purpose of postvention programs is to keep other teens
from attempting suicide. When unhappy teens hear of another
person dying by suicide, they may think it's okay to do the same
thing.

Sometimes, one or more teens who knew someone who killed
himself or herself decide to kill themselves. These are called
cluster suicides.

Researchers have found that people who die by suicide after an
initial suicide often felt alone with their problems. They saw
suicide as the only way out. That's why it's important for teens
who feel this way to seek professional help.

Counselors can give suicide survivors new ways to think about
suicide feelings. Survivors learn that suicide is part of a complex
process going on within the person who died. Survivors have
no control over this process. For this reason, suicide survivors
aren't to blame when others take their own life.

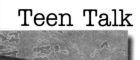

Copycat Suicides

Teens may consider a type of cluster suicide called copycat suicide. This occurs among people who don't know the person who initially killed himself or herself. For example, a teen may want to copy the suicide of a celebrity. A teen may think that all the attention from a suicide would be worth dying for. However, most teens aren't attracted to the idea of copycat suicide.

Some people blame the media for reporting suicides. These people believe that the reports give people ideas about killing themselves that they otherwise wouldn't have. Other people say media reports of the pain and despair of survivors can discourage thoughts of suicide. Media reports about a suicide can convince teens that suicide isn't for them.

Moving Through Grief

Learning to live without a person who has died by suicide is a slow process. The suicide survivor must find new ways to live without the person. This requires careful examination of your thoughts and feelings. It also means accepting that the suicide happened and learning to let go of the grief.

Letting go of grief is an important step in healing. Letting go does not mean forgetting. It means thinking of the person in a new way.

Sometimes suicide survivors find it difficult to let go of grief. Holding on to grief too long can be unhealthy. When too many bad feelings are stuffed into the body, it can overreact. Stomachaches, headaches, skin problems, or other painful results may occur. Unreleased grief can make the body seriously ill.

Unhealthy Grieving

Suicide survivors who are grieving in unhealthy ways may try to avoid other people. Sometimes they begin eating too much or too little. They may begin to abuse alcohol or other drugs. They may take unnecessary risks such as driving dangerously.

Panic attacks are another common occurrence for a suicide survivor. A panic attack fills a person with unexplained fear. Usually, there's no objective reason for the fear. The panic attack may last only a minute or two, but it may seem like hours.

Teen Talk

"I learned a lot from the counselor who came to our school when my friend Bobby tried to kill himself. Everyone asked the counselor a lot of questions about suicide. The principal was upset that the counselor allowed so many questions. I overheard the principal tell the counselor that he had caused a lot of problems. The counselor looked at the principal and said, 'The problems were already here. I just brought them to the surface.'"—Mohammad, age 15

The signs of a panic attack are:

o Heart beats faster and sometimes feels like it skips a beat.

o Head and hands may break out in a sweat.

o Skin may tingle.

o Head feels like it's in a tight band.

o Muscles knot up.

o Stomach muscles contract.

o Eyes see bright sparks.

o Head feels dizzy.

o Everything may go dark; may feel like you are going to faint.

o Stomach feels like you may throw up.

o Fear that you may die.

If you feel any of these panic attack symptoms, it's important to do the following:

- Take deep, slow breaths.

- Move the parts of your body around; swing arms out, kick with legs.

- Stay in the moment; don't think about anything else.

- Try not to ask questions like, "What if I pass out?"

- Stop yourself from thinking anxious thoughts.

Talk with a counselor or medical professional if you experience these panic attacks more than once or twice.

Relearning Life

As we live our life, we may take many things for granted. This may include what and when we eat or the time we spend with family. All of our activities and relationships are tied together. When someone dies by suicide, this pattern is broken. Everything is suddenly different.

The suicide survivor can find new ways to live without the person. When you begin to accept the loss, the work of rebuilding and relearning your life begins. Learning to live without the person who died by suicide is a slow process. It may take years. Relearning life does not mean you're through with grieving.

One decision becomes important at this time. It's the decision to choose to live again. That means going beyond your grief. The grief is still there, but it no longer rules your life. You can begin to do things in new ways.

Points to Consider

- What do you think when you hear or read about a teen dying by suicide?

- Do you think suicides should be reported in the media? Why or why not?

- Do you know of anyone who is grieving a suicide in an unhealthy way? If you don't know of anyone, have you seen movies or TV programs that have shown unhealthy grieving? How was the grieving unhealthy?

- What are some steps you think a person might take to relearn life?

Chapter Overview

- Only suicide survivors can do their own grieving. But loving friends can help a survivor through the grieving process.

- There are many ways to help a friend who is grieving the loss of someone to suicide. This chapter discusses several of them.

- Being an active listener is one of the best ways to help a grieving friend. An active listener must have empathy and the ability to be a word detective.

- It's helpful to give a grieving friend a journal to write feelings in. Helping him or her find a survivors' support group is another way to assist your friend.

- Helping a survivor can be difficult. It also can help you grow as a peron.

Helping a Suicide Survivor Heal

Only the survivor can do the hard work of grieving the loss of someone to suicide. But a loving family and friends can help. Being a friend to someone who is grieving takes courage. It also requires understanding and patience.

It may be hard to be a friend to a suicide survivor who is grieving. Survivors often feel confused. They may feel powerless, helpless, and separated from everyone. They may push friends away or tell others to mind their own business.

Did You Know?

Suicide survivor support groups and organizations can help people grieving someone's suicide. These groups can:

- Give suicide survivors a safe place to express feelings

- Be a source for finding new friends

- Help teens understand the complex feelings that a suicide survivor feels

- Help teens with their grief work

- Improve family relationships

Kevin and Derrik, Age 15

Kevin and Derrik had been best friends for years. When Kevin's 17-year-old brother Sam killed himself, Derrik wanted to help but wasn't sure how. Finally, he went to see the minister at his church, who gave him some good suggestions. His first suggestion was that Derrik get help with his own grief. "You can't give away what you don't have," he said. "If you don't deal with your own feelings, you can't help Kevin with his."

Every time Derrik tried to talk with Kevin, Kevin just ignored him. Finally, his persistence paid off as Kevin opened up about his feelings of anger and sadness about Sam.

Talking with someone is often helpful in dealing with your grief feelings. Find a family member, friend, or trusted adult who is willing to listen to you.

Suggestions for Helping a Friend Who Is Grieving

Derrik was glad that he talked with his minister before he visited Kevin. The minister gave him some good advice. Here are some of the things Derrik learned about helping a friend deal with grief:

- Your friend may resent you for trying to be part of his or her life at this time. Your friend may not even be aware of being rude.

- Be available to your friend whenever needed.

- Give constructive feedback only if your friend asks for it.

- Grief gets better after a while. A suicide survivor won't feel terrible forever. Try to stay optimistic until the survivor feels better.

- Grief numbs feelings. It may take some time before your friend gets past the confrontation phase.

- Help your friend work through grief one day at a time.

- If your friend begins to act in an unhealthy manner, tell a parent, teacher, or religious leader. You aren't betraying your friend.

Some experts believe that most people will have witnessed nearly 18,000 "deaths" by the time they are 18. These include fictional deaths on TV, in movies, and in books. It also includes death reports in news broadcasts.

- Listen actively.

- Never give advice unless your friend asks for it.

- No one can grieve for a suicide survivor, but just being there may help.

- Try to help your friend take small steps into the future.

- Understand that a grieving person hurts a great deal.

- Know when to leave your friend alone.

How to Listen Actively

Being an active listener is an important part of helping a suicide survivor through the grieving process. An active listener does more than just hear someone talk. An active listener pays attention to the grieving friend's words, emotions, and behaviors.

Two skills will help you be an active listener: having empathy and being a word detective.

Empathy is when you can feel what someone else is feeling. You might be able to do this by remembering feeling as your friend is feeling. This can help you understand your friend better.

A word detective hunts for clues about what the friend is really feeling. There are three ways to do this.

○ **Listen to what your friend is saying.** Concentrate completely. Don't think about what you will say next or about something unrelated to the discussion.

○ **Listen to what your friend is *not* saying.** Your friend may talk around the subject. You may feel the person is holding something back. You might want to make a guess: "It seems like you blame your dad for killing himself." Your friend will likely tell you if you're right or wrong.

○ **Listen for the words your friend selects.** These words can be translated into feelings. For example, your friend may say: "I have nothing to live for." This may mean: "Maybe I should kill myself, too."

A Gift Journal

A good gift to give a suicide survivor is a blank book to use as a journal. It's a place your friend can write down his or her feelings. Explain that journals are private. Also explain that the writing doesn't have to be perfect because no one else reads a private journal. These suggestions may help a suicide survivor begin writing in the journal:

○ Set aside special time when you won't be interrupted.

○ Write about anything you're feeling.

○ If you can't get started, try beginning a sentence with: "I'm remembering . . ." Do this whenever you get stuck.

○ Write without stopping for 10 or 15 minutes. Don't read it until the time is up. This may help you figure out what your deep, hidden feelings are.

Support Groups Can Help

You may want to suggest that your friend join a suicide survivors' support group. The people in a support group share similar grief feelings. Talking about suicide together often helps with working through the feelings. Offer to go with your grieving friend to the first meeting.

A Special Friend

It takes a special friend to help a suicide survivor through the grieving process. Being that friend can be difficult at times. It may stretch the friendship to the breaking point, but it also can strengthen the friendship. Helping a grieving suicide survivor may help you grow as a person.

Points to Consider

- In what ways would talking with a grieving friend be difficult?

- Have you ever tried to be an active listener? How did the other person respond?

- What are some ways you think you could help a suicide survivor who is grieving?

Note

At publication, all resources listed here were accurate and appropriate to the topics covered in this book. Addresses and phone numbers may change. When visiting Internet sites and links, use good judgment. Remember, never give personal information over the Internet.

Internet Sites

The Centre for Grief Education
www.grief.org.au/internetl.htm
Many links to grief and loss sites on the Internet

Counseling for Loss and Life Changes
www.counselingforloss.com
Links to other grief-related Internet sites

Death and Dying
www.death-dying.com/teen.html
Articles and a special chat rooms for teens

Suicide Awareness Voices of Education (SA\VE)
www.save.org
Facts about suicide and depression and information about suicide prevention

Hot Lines

Boys' Town Hot Line
Boys Town, NE 68010
1-800-448-3000

National AIDS Hot Line
1-800-342-AIDS (1-800-342-2437)

Youth Crisis Hot Line
1-800-HIT-HOME (1-800-448-4663)

In your local area, check the telephone listings under *Suicide* or *Suicide Survivors Support Groups* for names and phone numbers of agencies in your area that offer help or referral services.

Useful Addresses

American Association of Suicidology (AAS)
4201 Connecticut Avenue Northwest
Suite 408
Washington, DC 20008
www.suicidology.org
Clearinghouse on suicide information

Association for Death Education
and Counseling (ADEC)
342 North Main Street
West Hartford, CT 06117
www.adec.org
Promotes information on death education

Canadian Mental Health Association
2160 Yonge Street
Third Floor
Toronto, ON M4S 2Z3
CANADA
www.cmha.ca
Makes referrals for all types of loss

The Compassionate Friends
PO Box 3696
Oak Brook, IL 60522-3696
www.compassionatefriends.org
Many publications on losing a brother or sister

National Center for Death Education
New England Institute
Mount Ida College
777 Dedham Street
Newton, MA 02159

Teen Age Grief (TAG)
PO Box 220034
Newhall, CA 91322-0034
www.smartlink.net/~tag/info.html
Grief support for teens

For Further Reading

Kuehn, Eileen. *Loss: Understanding the Emptiness.* Mankato, MN:
    Capstone, 2001.

Peacock, Judith. *Teen Suicide.* Mankato, MN: Capstone, 2000.

Sprung, Barbara. *Death.* Austin, TX: Raintree Steck-Vaughn, 1998.

Woog, Adam. *Suicide.* San Diego: Lucent, 1997.

Glossary

accommodation (uh-kom-uh-DAY-shuhn)—the final phase of the grieving process; this is the slow acceptance of death on a day-to-day basis.

avoidance (uh-VOI-duhnss)—the first phase of the grieving process, in which a death is not acknowledged

bereavement (bi-REEV-muhnt)—shock and grief when a person dies

cluster suicide (KLUSS-tur SOO-uh-side)—a form of suicide that occurs when several people who knew a suicide victim decide to kill themselves, too

confrontation (kon-fruhn-TAY-shuhn)—the second phase of the grieving process, in which a person comes face-to-face with a death

cope (KOPE)—to struggle with and overcome something

denial (di-NYE-uhl)—not wanting to think about death or refusing to accept that a person has died

depressed (di-PRESST)—severely hopeless and sad

empathy (EM-puh-thee)—the ability to feel what someone else is feeling

funeral (FYOO-nuh-ruhl)—a ceremony for a dead person before burial

grieving (GREEV-ing)—a process of dealing with the deep feelings of a loss

post-traumatic stress disorder (POST-truh-MAT-ik STRESS diss-OR-dur)—feelings that occur long after a person has been exposed to violence or severe stress

postvention program (POST-ven-shuhn PROH-gram)—an organized program set up in schools or the community to help suicide survivors deal with their feelings

support group (suh-PORT GROOP)—a group of people who meet together to help each other with grief or other issues

Index

Index